Revolutionary Portraits ■ **William Shakespeare**

William Shakespeare

IN HIS TIMES, FOR OUR TIMES

Michael Rosen

REVOLUTIONARY PORTRAIT 5

William Shakespeare: in his times, for our times by Michael Rosen

Published in 2004 by

REDWORDS

1 Bloomsbury Street, London WC1B 3QE

www.redwords.org.uk

ISBN: 1 872208 18 5

Design and production: Roger Huddle and Hannah Dee

Printed by Cambridge Printing, Cambridge

Redwords is linked to Bookmarks the socialist bookshop

www.bookmarks.uk.com

CONTENTS

Introduction / 7

ONE   Romeo, Juliet and 20 cooks / 15

TWO   Cutting of throats / 29

THREE   Human nature (or, it's only natural) / 45

FOUR   Shakespeare today / 81

A note on books / 93

This book is in the series **Revolutionary Portraits** from Redwords. The unifying theme in this eclectic collection is the relationship between individual artists and larger historical forces, how each influences and shapes the other. All of the books in this series aim to lead us back to these works of art and music with new eyes and ears, and a deeper understanding of how art can raise the human spirit.

Redwords is a publishing collective specialising in art, history and literature from a socialist perspective.
We are linked to Bookmarks, the socialist bookshop.

Introduction

WE'RE SITTING IN A THEATRE and an old man, an aristocrat, steps forward and says in a state of distress:

'These late eclipses of the sun and moon portend no good to us... Love cools, friendship falls off, brothers divide; in cities mutinies, in countries discords, palaces treason, the bond cracked between son and father...the noble and true-hearted Kent banished, his offence honesty! 'Tis strange!'

[portend no good to us = indicate bad times ahead]

This is Gloucester. He turns and goes, leaving his bastard son Edmund to step forward.

(We already know of Edmund that he is plotting to get his father Gloucester to give him the ancestral land by disowning the legitimate son, Edgar.)

Edmund mocks his father's speech:

'This is the excellent foppery *[foolishness]* of the world: that when we are sick in fortune – often the surfeit *[excess]* of our own behaviour – we make guilty of our disasters the sun, the moon and the stars, as if we were villains by necessity, fools by heavenly compulsion, knaves, thieves and treacherers by spherical predominance, drunkards, liars and adulterers by an enforced obedience of planetary influence, and all that we are evil in, by a divine thrusting on. An admirable evasion of whoremaster man, to lay his goatish *[sexy]* disposition to the charge of stars. My father compounded *[had sex]* with my mother under the Dragon's tail and my nativity was under Ursa Major, so that it follows that I am rough and lecherous! Fut! I should have been that I am, had the maidenliest star of the firmament twinkled on my bastardy…'

So we are thrown into the middle of an intense struggle. At one level it's a battle for property, old aristocratic land. At another it's a struggle of ideas. The father, Gloucester, sees a changing world, a break-up of the established order at every level in society: personal – in matters of love or between, say, father and son; political – mutinies, treason; and ideological – 'discord'. The ultimate reason for this, he thinks, is the stars. The bastard son, Edmund, doesn't deny the description – after all, we know that he's the immediate cause of the discord and mutiny. But he debunks the cause and grabs us with what is, in effect, a materialist, atheist view of destiny. He tells us that he would have been what he is, no matter what star was twinkling at his birth.

This double punch, the mix of action and ideas, is what

makes Shakespeare such powerful stuff. We find ourselves in the midst of conflicts and confrontations; we are drawn into plotting and scheming carried out by people with ideas and opinions about other people's ideas. And they don't just mutter them to each other! They step forward and berate us with them, telling us what they are thinking at that very moment, in the midst of all the plotting and scheming.

Look how the rest of the scene unfolds.

Edgar, the legitimate son, enters and Edmund then pretends to be just the opposite of what he is: that he believes the stars *do* govern our lives. He delivers a speech that is really a send-up of what his father said earlier.

An authority on the stars has predicted, he says:
'unnaturalness between the child and the parent;
death, dearth, dissolutions of ancient amities,
divisions in state; menaces and maledictions against
king and nobles; needless diffidences, banishment of
friends, dissipation of cohorts *[bands of supporters]*,
nuptial breaches and I know not what.'

Edmund carries on conning his brother for a while until he's left alone on stage, and once again he steps forward to speak to us directly:
'A credulous father, and a brother noble,
Whose nature is so far from doing harms

That he suspects none; on whose foolish honesty
My practices ride easy. I see the business.
Let me, if not by birth, have lands by wit.
All with me's meet that I can fashion fit.'

[All with me's meet that I can fashion fit = anything I can utilise is fine by me]

Once again we have the double punch: in terms of the action, it's the father and brother's 'foolish honesty' that makes them gullible; in terms of the politics, we hear the materialist explanation that he'll get land 'by wit'. His own intelligence, cunning, skill and these alone – not the stars, not aristocratic inheritance – will lead him to have wealth. What's more, he'll employ any means necessary to do this. It's all fine by him. So we have confrontation, we have analysis, we have politics and we have ideas – all bubbling along at the same time.

This, then, is what we can expect from a Shakespeare play. And whether we're sitting in a theatre, watching a filmed version or reading it off the page, we can let our minds handle this in different ways. There's enough going on in a scene like the one I've just described to let it run as a struggle over property: the bad guy, con man, cynic getting the upper hand over old fogey good guys. Some might be content in feeling it in general, abstract terms as evil versus good. Whatever way we see it at first, it's exciting drama. My argument in this book, though, is that the more closely we look and listen to what's going on, another kind of power, a different kind of realism, appears.

So, yes, we're looking at evil and good, con-man son versus honest dad but, more specifically, we're looking at precisely the kind of conflict and confrontation that was going on in the society that Shakespeare lived in. An old aristocrat senses that the world is falling apart. A member of the new generation poses an alternative way of going on: you can do as well as the old aristocracy with their inherited wealth if you use your wit. So the old order is shown here as honest but doomed, and the new order is shown as dishonest, ruthless and greedy for power.

This struggle dominated the London society of Shakespearean times, and of course the rest of Europe. There are even glimpses of it in modern times in the struggles, say, in Margaret Thatcher's Tory party, between old wealth (Harold Macmillan style one-Britain politics) and new wealth (Norman Tebbit 'on yer bike', 'there's no such thing as society' politics); between the old-style patrician approach and the new, brash, loadsamoney outlook.

In Shakespeare's time this was a new and disturbing conflict. Many people in England lived in what were feudal or semi-feudal ways. An aristocratic master had rights over how you worked and where you lived. He could call on you for military service and demand that you appear in church on Sunday and on all holy days. In return, he was supposed to ensure that you didn't die of starvation and that if you had a son or daughter there was a possibility that he might employ them (or rape them) within his household. These feudal arrangements were by 1600 being torn down. You can hear Edmund describing this while pretending to be sorry about it in his speech to Edgar: 'dissolutions of ancient amities, divisions in state; menaces and maledictions against king and nobles'. Trade, manufacture and banking couldn't be held back by potentially loss-making, sentimental relationships. Just as the money-men say today, they have to be free to use anything and anyone for their ends: 'All with me's meet that I can fashion fit.'

In the London around Shakespeare's theatres this conflict of new versus old was only too apparent. The first banks and stock exchange had been built. Old aristocrats like the Roman Catholic Howard family from Norfolk had been thrust aside by newer wealth like the Protestant (some said 'atheist') Cecils, the power at the heart of Tudor and early Stuart England.

At the heart of many of Shakespeare's plays this conflict is there for us to see. In *The Merchant of Venice* we see a struggle between the old way of making money – small-time usury from Shylock – and the new way – speculating on colonial adventures from Antonio. In *Richard II* we see Bolingbroke seizing the crown because he deems the king unfit – so much for the 'divine right of kings'! We see people acting as 'Machiavels' – that's to say, like Machiavelli, the author of a book on how a ruler should govern by manipulation – people like Richard III, Iago in *Othello*, Claudius in *Hamlet*, Angelo in *Measure for Measure*, Don John in *Much Ado About Nothing*, Cassius in *Julius Caesar*, Juliet's father in *Romeo and Juliet* and, of course, Edmund who we've just seen in *King Lear*. These are all new men fighting to get their hands on the power once held by the old order.

Of course, Shakespeare's plays don't all follow this theme – they're full of fierce action and debate about, say, romantic love in *A Midsummer Night's Dream*, or pleasure in *Twelfth Night*. Specifically political themes about tyranny or power and colonialism are teased out in *Timon of Athens* and *The Tempest*. But these themes are not a matter of dry discussion. What we get with Shakespeare are the many viewpoints of a society in change. And the plays have a rich, diverse language to express this. They have the varying pace and methods of dialogue, soliloquy, poetry, prose, song, sideways comments to the audience from characters commenting on other characters and their actions – all of which keep an audience reflecting on what we see from different angles. This makes what we see and hear a dynamic process, just as the society Shakespeare lived in was one of dynamic change.

When we watch or read Shakespeare we can let our minds run between *(a)* feeling the characters as if they are real people, *(b)* making analogies with people we know, or know of, in our own lives, and *(c)* letting the plays work as if a wave of history was flowing over us.

In this book I want to look at *(1)* how a Shakespeare play works. I'm taking *Romeo and Juliet* as an example. I'll be looking at *(2)* the context in which Shakespeare wrote and *(3)* how this historical reality makes itself felt throughout the body of work. Finally I want to make a few comments on *(4)* Shakespeare today.

ONE: Romeo, Juliet and 20 cooks

ROMEO AND JULIET IS ONE of the best known of Shakespeare's plays. Film versions have reached millions of people, and it's been transformed into other kinds of entertainment, like ballet and opera. The name 'Romeo' has become a word in the English language, and a line like 'Romeo, Romeo, wherefore art thou Romeo?' is, if nothing else, a handy quote for a laugh. Others, like 'a plague on both your houses' (a slight misquote actually!) and 'parting is such sweet sorrow' have started to sound like proverbs, useful for slotting into conversations when the right time crops up.

Along with its ever-present position in English lessons, *Romeo and Juliet* has become a world icon. As such, it's one of the best examples of Shakespeare made safe. And yet in many ways it's just the opposite.

There's a lot of complicated activity in the play, including a crucial piece of bad luck, so it seems easy to talk about the play's 'Plot'. Most of the main people of the play – Romeo, Juliet, Juliet's father Capulet, Juliet's Nurse and Mercutio – seem simple to pluck off the page and describe as examples of what school exams call 'Character'. The play seems to have several beautifully described set pieces: the so-called 'Balcony Scene', Mercutio's 'Queen Mab' speech, and of course the linked deaths at the end of the play: Juliet's suitor Paris, Romeo and Juliet. In each of these there are speeches that are frequently isolated and pointed at as 'Great Poetry'. What's more, the play seems to repeat certain images, say, around the idea of lights at night, including stars – both in appearance and as astrological guides. This makes it ripe for the kind of talk about the play that treats it as if it's all a great big exercise in 'Imagery'. And then again, when it comes to talk of the play's 'Theme', the play seems to offer some people an excuse to get into hours of blathering about the mix of love and fate, and whether love tempts fate or fate tempts love, or total love is impossible because fate will intervene – and so on, and so on.

Romeo and Juliet need saving from a lot of this.

To see the play happen in front of you is to be thrown into a hectic series of events: quickfire entrances and exits, fights, rows, sharp dialogue. The unfolding of the play is not only speedy but done in rapid contrasts, intercutting between different and conflicting groups of people, rather like film and TV do today. Quite literally, we are one moment witnessing Friar Lawrence preparing Romeo and Juliet to marry, and the next a street fight in which Juliet's cousin Tybalt kills Romeo's friend Mercutio, followed straight after by Romeo killing Tybalt. When a scriptwriter looks at the play, one of the first things they notice is that it involves separate wheels of action: Romeo and Juliet falling in love, the street-fighting, Capulet's plans for Juliet to marry someone else. These wheels rotate separately but with rapid intercutting between the three.

This texture is part of the meaning of the play. In the same way that a cop series on the TV tries to capture the dynamism of, say, the New York streets, so *Romeo and Juliet* captures the impatience of the main characters: Romeo and Juliet to marry each other; Lord Capulet to get Juliet married off to a wealthy man of his choice; and the rich young men on the street out to better each other.

Now, leaving aside the main thrust of the storyline for the moment, the play shows us something else very interesting: all the various and many servants of the play, including Juliet's nanny and ex wet nurse ('Nurse'), keep up a riff of comments about their situations as servants to these masters and mistresses. Nurse remembers Juliet being a tetchy feeder on the breast; the musicians throw gags at each other about how they play for money; the house-servants are hard pressed when Capulet demands their labours in preparing for the two feasts he lays on. The very opening of the play shows Capulet's men saying, 'The quarrel is between our masters and us their men.' And the immediate cause of the lovers' deaths is a consequence of a servant or assistant (the Friar) not being able to deliver a letter. In other words, largely smothered by people gassing on about the play's poetry or the love/fate question, some kind of conversation is going on in the play about masters and servants.

What's this about? Sitting in the theatre, in a good production you are likely to see the main people of this drama – Capulet, Romeo, Juliet – always surrounded with some kind of cohort, a band of servants. It is an intrinsic part of their wealth that they can all command and order, and send people off to do things. There is an amazing moment of contrasts in the play, when Juliet concludes a highly dramatic, quiet conversation with the Friar (in which Juliet is going to take the death-dissembling potion) with the words 'Farewell, dear father' (a line usually taken to mean, farewell to the Friar). Then Juliet leaves. Quite literally, a second later, Juliet's real father rushes onto the scene with many others (in the setting of his own great house) calling out to a servant, 'Go hire me twenty cunning cooks.' Twenty? This is bigtime wealth. And if a writer wanted to highlight it, then hearing it straight after Juliet's quiet conversation with the Friar is as good a way as any. Earlier in the play we heard one of the servants describing him as 'the great rich Capulet'; Juliet's Nurse tells Romeo that the man who can marry Juliet will come in for 'chinks', ie, plenty of money; and the opening line of the whole play is 'Two households, both alike in dignity...' where we can take dignity to mean 'rank' or 'status', linking their wealth to some kind of official acknowledgement.

At one point there is real conflict over the rights of master over servant when Nurse demands the right to speak on Juliet's behalf.

'You are to blame, my lord,' she says to Capulet, 'to rate her so.' *[to berate her]*

He sneers back sarcastically: 'And, why, my Lady Wisdom? Hold your tongue,

Good Prudence. Smatter with your gossips, go!' *[chatter with your cronies]*

To which she replies bravely and dangerously, 'I speak no treason.'

'O, God-I-god-en.' *[meaning here 'Get on with you' or 'God save us!']*

'May not one speak?' says she.

'Peace, you mumbling fool!

Utter your gravity o'er a gossip bowl,

For here we need it not.'

Sex, slang and disobedience!

Does this relate to the meat of the play or is it simply there, as critics used to say, as some kind of populist sop to the working class element in the original audience? Is it there as some kind of 'relief' from the high tension of what's happening to Romeo and Juliet? My view is that the main drama of the play shows us a class of people in action – the new class appearing in Shakespeare's London, the rich urban families. A writer has various ways of showing that. Here it's done to a great degree through the involvement of servants. What with Nurse's rude but real chat about sex, or the musicians' talk about playing for money, or the house-servants rushing about to arrange their master's feasts, these servants show us:

– the reality that lies beneath their masters' and mistresses' lives;

– an earthy realism about sex, childcare and real labour – in contrast to the high romantic love of Romeo and Juliet, and the materialist, power-seeking attitude towards arranged marriage of the Capulets;

– how necessary they, the servants, are for all the daily arrangements to happen. (For Romeo and Juliet to sleep together, it is Nurse who has to fetch a rope ladder to throw over the orchard wall.)

In other words the servants, again and again in the play, are significant 'agents'. They enable things to happen.

Now, it's my view that this aspect of the play supports the core. So, what is the core?

If, as some do, we simply lift the phrase from the opening of the play that this Shakespeare play is a story of two 'star-crossed lovers', then we miss crucial aspects of the play. We miss the social commentary that runs through the play:

– the conflict between *(a)* giving rein to real feelings (Juliet's outlook) and *(b)* wealth- and power-preservation in rich families (Juliet's father's outlook);

– the lawlessness of the men in high-ranking families;

– the absolutism of a ruler;

– the inability of formal religion to offer absolute rules on real social and personal affairs (the Friar's situation);

– the consequences for servants when masters enlist them in their disputes; the consequences for masters of relying on servants to convey their messages.

Now, in the popular mind, the reason why Romeo and Juliet never manage to live happily ever after is because they come from opposing families – opposing sides, if you like. I would suggest that this may well be the shell of the story, but the core is different.

Firstly, the context: a cluster of rich young men, fully armed, apparently able and ready to kill each other. The Shakespearean era is marked by almost permanent war. One of the consequences of this was that there was a permanent layer of rich young men either waiting to be blooded in combat, just back from combat or, of course, dead. Here's Mercutio in top flight jokingly describing the effect that the queen of the fairies has on people:

'Sometime she driveth o'er a soldier's neck,

And then dreams he of cutting foreign throats,

Of breaches, ambuscadoes, Spanish blades,
Of healths, five fathoms deep; and then anon
Drums in his ear, at which he starts and wakes,
And being thus frighted, swears a prayer or two
And sleeps again.'

[healths, five fathoms deep = toasting someone while drowned five fathoms down]

In some ways, the tribal loyalty issue of the two families in feud is less important than the simple fact that what we see are groups of rich young men with their servants wanting to kill each other. It's often overlooked that the cause of the first street murder (which then causes the others) is *not* a Montague v Capulet row. It's because Mercutio (who belongs to neither family) is angered that Romeo (a Montague) won't take on Tybalt (a Capulet): 'O vile submission.' (Interestingly enough on this matter of servants and masters, the pre-fight war-words involve Mercutio taking umbrage over being told that he is Romeo's servant.)

In my mind, the first reason that the time and space are wrong for Romeo and Juliet to fulfil their love is a political one: because rich young men are armed, skilled and idle.

The second real reason for the relationship to end in disaster comes in the scene where Capulet tells Juliet that she must marry his protégé, Paris.

At this point in the play our heads are full of the things we've seen and heard, such as:

– the Prince passing his edict that people who fight in

the streets do so on pain of death;

– Romeo's friend Mercutio stabbed to death by Juliet's cousin, Tybalt;

– Tybalt stabbed to death by Romeo;

– Romeo and Juliet secretly married;

– Juliet's father, Capulet, coming to an agreement with Paris about when he is going to marry Juliet;

– Romeo and Juliet secretly spending the night together in Capulet's house;

– Romeo slipping away to exile in Mantua.

We have witnessed a socially constructed community:

– rich people with their servants;

– political edicts about the civil order;

– personal edicts about arranged marriage;

– as well as a great deal of talk and humour about love and sex, including the strange mock-religious moment of Romeo and Juliet's first meeting and kissing.

All this has passed in front of us before we see Juliet bundling Romeo out the window out the back (thanks to Nurse) after her first night of sex with a man.

The next second she is thrust into a conversation with her mother and father – a conversation that we know (from what's preceded it) is going to be about marrying Paris. This is a classic Shakespearean moment in that what we the audience know is more than what the people on the stage know. So Capulet doesn't know that Juliet is in love, is married to Romeo, or indeed that she has had sex with him. We do. Juliet doesn't know that Capulet has stitched it up that she should marry Paris. We do. This is yet another way in which watching a Shakespeare play is dynamic.

To continue, the central conflict in the scene is between Juliet and her father. Though the play is cast as a conflict between two families, it's crucial to the scene that the reason for this row is *not* that Juliet is in love with someone from the rival family. Capulet doesn't know that. It is because she wants to defy his demands for an arranged marriage. In other words, the issue in his eyes is not that she is in love with this or that person, Montague or not, but simply that she will not marry his protégé. The fact that we know she is in love, is married, has had sex (all with a member of the rival family) is in our heads, not Capulet's.

So this is a scene about the absolute power of a rich family patriarch: analogous to (and perhaps part of) the absolute power of the Prince in his dictatorial rule over the city where they live. What is also interesting in the scene is that there is a conflict between two outlooks, not simply a conflict of characters. Juliet's outlook is clearly that she is entitled to pursue her emotional life. Capulet's outlook is that he is the one who has the power to determine who Juliet should marry and that this is a socioeconomic matter. Paris, significantly, is a kinsman of the absolute Prince who rules the city. The Capulets would be doing very well by marrying into the social layer immediately above them. Lady Capulet elsewhere in the play points out that the wealth of the two families is well matched. This is a picture of what was happening to the new rich in Shakespeare's time. They were constantly trying to find ways to lever themselves up a notch, ideally into the aristocracy, and marriage was a perfect way to do it. Such a 'marrying up' would have been instantly recognisable to Shakespeare's audience.

This matter of conflicts of outlook is one of the key aspects of Shakespearean drama that the great suffocation machine has done so well to reduce and eliminate. By elevating all the talk of Character, the imagery of Language and the great generalised blather of Theme, it becomes very easy to squeeze out this matter of how the characters have social and ideological outlooks. Listen to Capulet:

'...get thee to church a Thursday   *[ie to marry Paris]*
Or never after look me in the face.'
Speak not, reply not, do not answer me.
My fingers itch.'   *[ie he wants to hit her]*

So, do what I say or I'll disown you (in a society with very little social care provision this means destitution, as will be underlined a moment or two later).

Then:

'It makes me mad.

Day, night; hour, tide, time; work, play:
Alone, in company, my care hath been
To have her matched; and having now provided
A gentleman of noble parentage,

[demesnes =
domains,
property]

Of fair demesnes, youthful and nobly trained…
And then to have a wretched puling fool…

[puling =
whining]

To answer "I'll not wed"…'

So he is saying it makes him furious that he has done all he can to match Juliet in terms of property.

Then comes what, for me, is one of the crucial moments in the play – if Juliet won't do what he says and marry Paris on Thursday:

'Graze where you will, you shall not house with me…

[And = if]

And you be mine, I'll give you to my friend;
And you be not, hang, beg, starve, die in the streets,
For by my soul, I'll ne'er acknowledge thee.'

Juliet, remember, by this time in the play has already expressed herself as a clear-minded, witty, clever lover, able to exert her will over Romeo, demanding from him seriousness, while expressing her absolute and total passion. She has shared her body with him…she has 'known a man', as people used to say. And here is her father saying, 'I'll give you to my friend.' What a powerful and crucial contrast, again, of outlook.

And what is he threatening her with? A situation utterly

real to that audience as it walked out of the theatre into the 'infested tenements' of Shoreditch: begging, starving and dying in the streets. The years that this play was first put on were full of people begging, starving and dying in the streets – whether it was for reasons of terrible harvests or massive plague, or the consequences of wars in Ireland and the Low Countries, decimating in particular the population of wage-earning men, thereby depriving their dependants (the old, child-bearing women, and children) of food and shelter.

He says, 'I'll ne'er acknowledge thee.' In other words, he'll disown her utterly. Capulet's wife goes along with this even when Juliet threatens suicide. In some ways it's a disgusting picture of the self-importance and authoritarianism of the rich. In others it shows what their attitude is to the individual's right to express themselves, and again it shows how it's not sufficient for them to own property (and, as we see elsewhere, the labour of others), but it's also necessary for them to own the bodies of their wives and daughters.

So if we ask that old corny question, 'Why do Romeo and Juliet die?' one of the key answers is that it's because Juliet has to marry who Capulet wants her to marry. Again, this is not simply or only a matter of the old rivalry between the two families, but purely a question of Capulet's absolute requirement that she marry his choice of partner. And this is how a rich family keeps or

TWO: 'Cutting of throats'

A STRANGE PART OF THE Shakespeare industry is that although the icon of Shakespeare is forever being connected to material things – like the old school in Stratford where Shakespeare probably went to school, or the Globe Theatre in Southwark, London – much less noise is made about, say, the wars, conspiracies, plotting and spying that went on in Shakespeare's time. It's not as though these upheavals are merely some kind of backdrop to the plays. Many of the best known – *Julius Caesar*, *Macbeth*, *King Lear*, *Henry IV Part One* and *Part Two*, *Hamlet*, *Richard II*, *Richard III* – have these matters at their heart.

The same again could be said of the changing conditions for the old rich, the new rich and the ever-present poor. These too step out in front of us in, say, *King Lear*, the Henry plays, *Measure for Measure*, *The Merchant of Venice*, and so on.

The Shakespeare industry doesn't usually spend too much time filling us in with a sense of how the layers of society in Shakespeare's time lived and engaged with each other. In fact, with all the emphasis on 'Character', it's not often that we see a sideways slice through the plays taken on the basis of social position and class, like this, say:

– *the so-called 'middling sort'* that we find in Shakespeare: lesser gentry like Toby Belch, Andrew Aguecheek (both from *Twelfth Night*), Capulet from *Romeo and Juliet*, and John Falstaff and the Justice of the Peace Shallow along with the money-men Antonio and Shylock of *The Merchant of Venice*;

– *power-hungry, manipulative men* in the layer just below the monarchy, who may or may not become rulers: Edmund the bastard in *King Lear*, Bolingbroke in *Richard II*, conspirators like Brutus and Cassius in *Julius Caesar*, the stand-in ruler, Angelo, in *Measure for Measure*; Richard III himself, Claudius in *Hamlet*, Don John in 'Much Ado About Nothing';

– *advisers and confidants* in service to people with power like Polonius in *Hamlet*, Iago in *Othello*;

– *intellectual aristocrats* such as Hamlet, Benedick and Beatrice in *Much Ado About Nothing*, Prospero in *The Tempest*;

– *women exerting direct and indirect power* at the top of the hierarchy or just below it: Cleopatra, Lady Macbeth, Goneril and Regan from *King Lear*, Gertrude from

Hamlet, Titania in *A Midsummer Night's Dream*;

   – *local aristocratic or rich 'middling' women* like Olivia and Viola in *Twelfth Night* or Portia from *The Merchant of Venice*, Hermia and Helena in *A Midsummer Night's Dream*;

   – *the artisans, servants and labourers* such as the rebels of *Coriolanus* and *Henry VI*, the slaves in *The Tempest*, the tavern gang of *Henry IV*, the 'rude mechanicals' of 'A *Midsummer Night's Dream*, the network of servants in *Romeo and Juliet*.

And yet in simply and crudely listing these social layers like this, it's not easy to give these roles their dynamism. That's to say, all these people are involved in what can be called 'activity': planning, scheming and changing their circumstances, pursuing intentions and facing consequences. What we see in Shakespeare are social beings in action, and (most importantly and so often ignored) it is the consequences of these people's outlooks – in their changing social positions – that so often provide the meat of the drama. To take the example of *The Merchant of Venice* – do we regard it as a conflict between, say, a lonely bachelor and a rapacious unforgiving Jew? Or do we see it as the working through in personal terms of a social conflict between two outlooks: that's to say, two ways of making money, the old (usury) and the new (venture capital)?

And, we can add here, the very fact that we see any people below the level of the monarchy, outside of biblical or classical stories, trying to determine and alter their own destiny is itself a statement on changing times, a change in power relations in Shakespeare's society, and a change in a sense of self at that time.

Again, when we read that the language of the plays is so profuse and various (and all the offputting idolatry that goes with this) it is not simply because Shakespeare and his co-writers and performers were supremely clever. It is that the language proliferates and dazzles as it tries to grasp the changing circumstances, the diversity and the complexity of these beings in society ('characters' so called), these real human beings in change, real human beings in action. One way this complexity is grasped is through the 'soliloquy', when we hear people thinking aloud. Another is through the effect of hearing people commenting on others' behaviour. And yet another is through interlocking storylines that work off against each other, as you find in, say, *A Midsummer Night's Dream*.

The creators of the Shakespeare plays (generally presumed to be Shakespeare as main scriptwriter working with a team of actors, directors and various co-writers) lived and worked through a time of upheaval, conflict, danger, difficulty, change and innovation. Because the figure of Elizabeth I was then and is still today so dominant, it's easy to be lulled into a sense of the era as another bit of 'merrie England', with jolly sea dogs singeing the King of Spain's beard, the queen not being able to make up her mind about who to marry, Sir Walter Raleigh smoking a pipe and eating spuds (at the same time?), much rollicking and roistering in taverns, creepy ghosts in the Tower of London, and so on…

Shakespeare himself has been recruited for this representation, as many of the plays are full of song and dance, gags, uplifting and uniting conclusions in marriage, seeing off of unsavoury rulers, foreigners and rebels – an event usually followed by hopeful wishes that life will be better now. And, clearly, his plays and theatre (he co-owned the Globe) along with the other theatres and plays of the time were part of the way in which the people of that time made their lives more enjoyable, and perhaps more 'merrie'.

The problem though is that it becomes very difficult to relate all this jollity with what we see in front of us in many of the plays. Hamlet knows that his father was killed by the man who is now king. This murderer is the old king's brother and has now married Hamlet's mother. This isn't just a bit of jiggery-pokery. It is, just as the quote says, something rotten in the state of Denmark. The *state*. And not very merrie it is. King Lear can't get a bed to sleep in for the night because his daughters and their husbands, who've taken power, won't give him house room. Macbeth, a nobleman, murders the king in order that he will become king, and, as we hear from a couple of characters, the whole country is falling apart. Brutus, Cassius and the other leading politicians kill a great general, Julius Caesar, because they think he wants to become king. A usurer and a merchant haggle to the death (or very nearly) over legitimate ways of keeping to financial agreements in *The Merchant of Venice*. In *The Tempest*, a deposed and seemingly powerless aristocrat uses his brain to try and control everything in his known world. Various rulers and powerful people try to control the sex lives of people less or more powerful than they – Angelo in *Measure for Measure*, Oberon in *A Midsummer Night's Dream*, Capulet in *Romeo and Juliet*, Iago in *Othello*. A debate about love, pleasure and sex goes on in several of the plays like, say, *Much Ado About Nothing* and *Twelfth Night*. Frequently, but not always, the efforts to control sex and pleasure rebound on the person(s) trying to do the controlling.

All this is very hard to relate to a simple, jolly picture of merrie England, or for that matter to the sight, say, of Shakespeare's 'second best bed' – bequeathed to his wife in his will, and there in reality today, so it's claimed, in Stratford.

So, how to grasp Shakespearean times?

Shakespeare died in 1616 at the age of 52, so the last 13 years of his life were spent living in James I's time. When we bear in mind that his successful play-writing couldn't have begun much before 1590, it follows in time terms alone that he's as much a 'Jacobean' playwright as 'Elizabethan'. Or, at the very least, the first part of his writing life comes at the end of Elizabeth's reign. I say this as a reminder that Shakespeare's play-writing spans a time of great uncertainty and anxiety about how the society Shakespeare lived in was to be ruled. This is not really a matter of differing personalities of real and/or potential rulers – 'Elizabeth was wise, James was foolish', that sort of thing. It is something deeper and more complex than that. One of the most difficult things to understand about how countries were run 400 years ago is how they were really ruled.

At one level, monarchs like Elizabeth and James had immense power. Nothing could be law unless they signed the paper. All the many executions, engaging in wars, levying of taxes, the right to engage in certain kinds of business, the right to explore this or that part of the globe, who ruled in the countryside, who ran the church – all required the signature of the monarch. But unlike the picture given to us in recent TV accounts, this power wasn't exercised merely as an extension of the monarch's personality. It was exercised in conjunction with a group of the country's most powerful men. Essentially, this was the 'Privy Council', an inner cabinet that still exists today.

So the Shakespearean period sees the Cecil family

(father and then son) dominant in this Privy Council, pursuing a policy of ruthless imposition of Crown authority. They demanded that everyone signed up to their version of royally sanctioned Christianity – 'English Protestantism' – and persecuted (ie spied on, tortured and killed) anyone who didn't conform: Roman Catholics on one side and 'Puritans' on the other. This persecution goes on in the context of wars, piracy and colonialism abroad and the rise of the new banking-merchant-manufacturing class at home. As a very broad generalisation, the old landed aristocracy, in particular in the north and west of England, was likely to cling secretly to Roman Catholicism, while the new urban middle class of London and the wealthy non-aristocratic farmers of the south and east were likely to be loyal and Protestant. The tendency to throw off all priestly authority, the various strains of Puritanism – Quakers, Anabaptists and the like – were a small but growing tendency among the new middle classes, artisans and immigrant refugees from the Low Countries.

Meanwhile, the pressure put on rural labourers, small farmers, artisans, waged workers, apprentices, servants and the unwaged (the old, infirm, childbearing women, disabled and the like) was in many places and for much of the time immense. Throughout Shakespeare's life there were riots and rebellions both in the countryside and in the city. Indeed, right on his doorstep in Stratford the town council asked Shakespeare to support them in their opposition to the local aristocrat enclosing common land, and again on his other doorstep, next to the Globe theatre, the local weavers rioted against the foreign weavers who they claimed were undercutting their wages. Meanwhile, the wars and piracy pursued by the Elizabethan regime slaughtered thousands, injured hundreds of thousands, and created a permanent state of tyranny and spying around recruitment, mutiny and desertion.

This then is a time of conflicts and struggles, and Shakespeare's plays are brimful of it all. The plays look again and again at what might be called 'governance'. What is the best way to run a society? Should monarchs who abuse their power be removed? What is power? Should power be delivered by those who inherit it or by some other means? He looks at the outlooks of people in the different positions and layers of society going through upheavals, conflicts and plotting. Though at first glance the plays are at several removes from Elizabethan England – old English history, Ancient Rome, Venice, Illyria, ancient Scotland, Denmark – it's clear that the meat of the plays refer back to and reflect very directly on Shakespeare's times.

What's more, he seems particularly interested in the ways in which people in their differing social positions express their feelings – in particular, but by no means only, love for the opposite sex. As we've seen, Juliet's father doesn't seem to acknowledge that love and passion between a man and a woman exists. Or if it does, it should be overlooked for reasons of money and status. The marriage contract is to him a business contract. On the other hand, the high-flown, classical love-talk of Romeo in particular is frequently punctured either by Juliet or by the undercurrent of sexual gags from, say, the Nurse. In fact, though the plays are popularly loved for their high-flown love chat, over and over again, in plays like *Twelfth Night* or *A Midsummer Night's Dream*, this is undermined and mocked. On the other hand, figures like Richard III and Angelo in *Measure for Measure* believe they can force women to be their sexual partners by virtue of their status; while we see, in the Macbeths' marriage and the Claudius-Gertrude marriage in *Hamlet*, or Coriolanus and his mother, a picture of an unholy alliance, the conspiratorial state-seizing relationship.

And Shakespeare seems particularly interested in whether it is possible for people to change their lives and the lives of others. Are there limits to the power people have over others? And is it all governed by the stars, God's divine will, or Fate, anyway? Macbeth is told by the Witches (people who know what our fate is) that he will be king, but he grabs the crown by his own deeds. Iago in *Othello* discovers that through his actions he can bring down the most powerful man in the city. Bolingbroke in *Richard II* and the senators in *Julius Caesar* find that they can seize state power through assassination, Hotspur in

Henry IV Part One and, as we've seen, Edmund in *King Lear* defy the stars to pursue their intentions.

When it comes to love, a group of young lovers in *Much Ado About Nothing* find out that they can will two people to love each other, by laying a plot; Cleopatra in *Antony and Cleopatra* is a powerful and sexy woman who can exert control over men but in the final analysis can't pull the same tricks on a ruthless, power-hungry general. As an intellectual, Hamlet can see quite clearly that the state has been seized by a murderer but finds it impossible on his own to find a way to reform or change things.

All this plotting and scheming, all these efforts, successful or not, to secure outcomes are in a way part of the story of the Shakespearean era.

At a military and political level, the two regimes of Shakespeare's lifetime were full of plots and counterplots. The Tudors, after all, had a very shaky hereditary claim to the throne. The old aristocracy with its Roman Catholic leanings were finding that their power base was under threat from new wealth, whether it came from the new farming rich or from the mercantile-manufacturing-banking rich. So, as one example, a military adventurer-aristocrat like the Earl of Essex put himself, very late on in Elizabeth's reign, at the head of a rebellion against the throne. The war with Spain, taking place in the Low Countries, Ireland and at sea, was in reality a civil war too, with the Elizabethan regime taking on Roman Catholics everywhere.

At an intellectual level, the era explodes with a different kind of scheming: the generation of new ideas, scientific discoveries, historical discoveries through old manuscripts, research and creativity. Instead of intellectual speculation being restricted to the church, this period marks the coming of age of the non-ecclesiastical thinker – people like Francis Bacon, Walter Raleigh and less well-known people like the parliamentarian Peter Wentworth, who were starting to challenge the Crown's power. This occurs just as the state-sanctioned pirates, adventurers and colonists like Francis Drake and Martin Frobisher unleash themselves on the non-European world and on any other European power that stands in their way.

Up to this time, most intellectuals had argued their position through the medium of religion. For nearly a hundred years Europe had been rocked by the upheaval known as the 'Reformation'. If nothing else, this reveals to everyone in society that Christianity is not one monolithic truth. By Shakespeare's time it had become a global contest. In truth, the English state's Protestant version of Christianity wasn't so very different in religious terms from Rome's. However, it was nationally distinct. That's to say it was run by the English state and not from Rome. This nationalism is supported by the long-awaited and officially sanctioned translation of the Bible into English.

It was in Shakespeare's own lifetime that the Bible became available to everyone either to read or hear in English. People didn't have to wait for a priest, a monk or a nun to tell them what the Bible was about.

This is one context for the outbreak of a pamphlet war that runs simultaneously with Shakespeare's writing and right through to the outbreak of a real war, the English Revolution. It had always been the case for those maintaining the status quo, the power of the monarchy and the like, to support themselves with what was supposed to be God's word or will. Now it was possible for anyone, any group, any political movement or religious sect to lay claim to this or that passage of the Bible to support their demands. 'Blessed are the meek for they shall inherit the earth,' the dispossessed could now shout, interpreting 'meek' as 'poor'.

In a physical way, things were changing too: the new rich, learning a trick or two from the old aristocracy, were rushing to put up mansions in the country and city; big landowners who held the ancient title to common land were trying to kick the peasantry off these 'commons'; London, with its three miles' worth of docks, was becoming the trading centre for developing mercantile capitalism in the colonial 'new world'. It was expanding at a massive rate, sucking in foreign workers, dispossessed land-workers and ex-soldiers. Ramshackle multi-occupied tenements were going up all round the fringes of the City, exactly where Shakespeare's theatres were – Shoreditch and Bankside.

A close look at the records finds, in this time, apprentices rioting, rebellions over enclosures taking place all over the country, and the first executions of Puritans for not accepting either the old Roman Catholic, aristocratic power structure, or the Tudor and Stuart version of state religion and power. In 1596, about the time Shakespeare wrote *Romeo and Juliet*, *A Midsummer Night's Dream* and *The Merchant of Venice*, a note was passed to the queen from the Privy Council warning her that this year 'will be the hardest year for the poor in man's memory' and that as a result there would be 'cutting of throats'.

All this meant that people were discovering a basic human truth: that human beings make history. This was by no means self-evident. In medieval times the central plank of popular belief rested on a strange combination of pagan, classical and Christian ideas that together take responsibility of existence away from humans and hand it over to the stars, the planets, God, fate and, in some cases, spirits and fairies. Shakespeare marks a point of dawning, a moment when people realise that, say, wealth was something you could acquire through trade not by inheritance; that you could gain high office without being born into it; that money could open almost any door you want; and that love is not easily restrained by power. What is surprising, sometimes stunning, is how often the plays show the detail and complexity of all this – which I'll turn to now.

THREE: Human nature (or it's only natural)

IN THIS CHAPTER I WOULD like first to go back to *King Lear*, the play I mentioned in the introduction.

Listening to radio phone-ins and reading the tabloids, it's not long before we come across the phrase 'human nature', or 'it's only natural'. There is, in a way, an informal popular religion that runs alongside the sets of rules that are laid down in, say, the Bible. You can hear people justify a whole range of actions on the grounds that it's natural – jealousy, motherly love, women's ability to iron clothes, men getting drunk, competitive exams, thinking that beautiful people are clever, living in families, hanging out with people who have the same skin colour as you, slapping children, wanting murderers to be executed and admiring the Windsors. Not that these ideas go uncontested. Some people will argue with them by quoting religious texts like 'love thy neighbour' while others, like me, use examples from anthropology, psychology, and the long history of revolt and resistance. This debate doesn't go on isolated from the people making the arguments. With Thatcherism in its heyday, the airwaves were full of successful people using nature to justify how life is really about competing against others, beating them and 'looking after your own'. The 1984-5 miners' strike was, in some ways, a struggle against this. Miners had long worked in ways that involved another set of ideas – looking out for each other, creating better conditions for yourself by taking action together (one for all, all for one), and running local and national organisations in a democratic, collective way. With the strike, the miners brought in millions of other people – workers, students, retired workers, the unemployed and the like – to see that this wasn't only a fight about miners' jobs but also about what kind of society we wanted to live in. Should it be based on profit (and competition) or based on everyone's needs (and cooperation)? Through the miners' action and the support they got, many of the ideas about what's natural were defied.

In Shakespeare's time the arguments about human nature broke out along different lines, though we inherit some of these today. There was a traditional, late medieval view which held that there was a divine order to nature and this was for everyone's good. Everything in the cosmos, in the natural world (flowers, animals, sea, mountains) and in society was all ordered the way it was because that was the natural order. Whether it was a downpour of rain, the appointment of bishops, the taking of tithes from the peasants, capital punishment, charity, hereditary kingship – it was all natural and all, in the end, for the good. Through the 16th and 17th centuries several alternatives to this view emerge. One says, yes, there is a natural state of human existence, but that isn't what it's like. Nature is, as it were, Thatcherite – human beings are governed by personal desire and self-interest. As you might imagine, this means that there is a debate about which of these two models of nature is preferable, what the consequences are, whether they can be blended.

Though it's essayists, writers, clerics and academics who engage in the debate, the debate isn't purely academic. There for all to see and experience were real people acting out their lives along the principles that were being argued about. Take landowners: one group acted along feudal lines, taking, from the peasants under their sway, percentages of their crops and livestock production, pressing them into military, domestic and sexual service, while 'giving back' rights to graze their animals on the common land and offering them 'protection' against attackers. This was in their eyes natural, divinely ordered and for the general good. A new group of landowners broke with this pattern, moved across to a cash-based economy selling, say, wool, by taking over the strips of peasant land plus the common land, and employing (or other? At the heart of Elizabethan government, this argument was given life by the presence of *(1)* a monarchy cult around Elizabeth herself – representing, in a way, the old argument about the natural divine order, and *(2)* a ruthless, cunning, manipulative Privy Council that waged the wars, levied the taxes, granted the monopolies, controlled the circulation of the printed word, ordered executions and ran the spy network – representing the new argument.

Bearing all this in mind, let's look again at *King Lear*.

In the introduction we already heard from Gloucester and his bastard son Edmund, but it's a play with a double storyline. One concerns King Lear, a king of ancient England, who has three daughters, Goneril, Regan and Cordelia. Lear states that he intends to 'shake all cares and business from our age, conferring them on younger strengths, while we, unburthen'd *[unburdened]* crawl towards death'. He's going to retire. This means that he'll give his daughters and their husbands, present or future, proportions of the kingdom. *What* proportions depend, says Lear, on which of the daughters will say she loves him the most. Goneril and Regan show themselves to be expert in flattering the old king, while Cordelia says that she has nothing to say other than that she loves Lear according to her 'bond'.

'Good my Lord,
You have begot me, bred me, lov'd me: I

Return those duties back as are right fit,
Obey you, love you and most honour you.'

In other words Shakespeare shows us Cordelia putting her love for her father solidly into the *old* idea of nature: the natural order, based on lifetime bonds and duties returned to those who begot you. Yet the consequences for Cordelia are that she is dispossessed, given away to the King of France and banished. When Lear's faithful aristocratic servant, Kent, pleads with Lear that he's doing the wrong thing, Kent himself is banished as well. The parallel storyline, as we've seen, concerns Gloucester and his two sons, one legitimate, the other a bastard. The play is the agonised working through of *(1)* the consequences of Lear's actions in the scene I've just recounted until he can be reunited with Cordelia and the outlook I've just quoted her expressing; and *(2)* the determination of bastard Edmund to get his hands on wealth and power. What's more, the play returns again and again to the issue of what kind of sex and what kind of break in well-ordered nature went to produce the bastard in the first place.

What we see unfold in front of us are some of the most curious, savage and pitiful scenes ever to be written for the theatre. First, let's return to Edmund. We've already seen him conning his father and brother. In actual fact, his first appearance is in some ways even more stunning. Imagine a young, energetic, sexy man walking down to the front of the stage and talking straight at you and the rest of the audience. Perhaps he takes a look at you all and then addressing no one in particular but the world in general he says:

'Thou, Nature, art my goddess; to thy law
My services are bound. Wherefore should I
Stand in the plague of custom, and permit
The curiosity of nations to deprive me,
For that I am some twelve or fourteen moonshines
Lag of a brother?'

['stand in the plague of custom' = be dependent on bothersome custom]

['curiosity of nations' = the old laws of nations with their silly distinctions]

['moonshines lag of' = behind in months]

In saying all this in his opening speech, we see Edmund as being part of the new order, the new outlook on nature. Some have claimed even more: that by saying Nature is his 'goddess', he is saying that he is outside of religion and the old laws of society – the very accusation levelled by the old order at Elizabeth's ruling elite.

Edmund goes on talking about himself (who else!):
'Why bastard? Wherefore base?
When my dimensions are as well compact,
My mind as generous and my shape as true
As honest madam's issue? Why brand they us
With base? With baseness? Bastardy? Base, base?'
(Our sexy young man will be savouring these words, savouring the shock that this has on his audience.)
'Who in the lust stealth of nature take
More composition and fierce quality

[bastards were usually called vile, base, low, etc]

Than doth within a dull, stale, tired bed
Go to th'creating a whole tribe of fops,
Got 'tween asleep and wake?'
(So he reckons that he's got more worth in him because his parents had sex in a lusty way (ie with 'natural' appetites) rather than the ordered way of arranged marriages, dutiful sex, creating, he claims, a class of 'fops', ie, fools in Shakespearean English.)
'Well then,
Legitimate Edgar, I must have your land;
Our father's love is to the bastard Edmund
As to th'legitimate. Fine word, "legitimate"!
Well, my legitimate, if the letter speed,
And my invention thrive, Edmund the base
Shall top th'legitimate. I grow, I prosper;
Now, gods, stand up for bastards!'

It's a fantastic speech, every word can be savoured and punched home. Look at those words 'invention', 'thrive', 'grow', 'prosper'. They are the meat and potatoes of the new ideology, supporting the new class. And they come out of the mouth of a man who, as we see later in the play, has no compunction about lying, cheating and conning everyone he meets. Everything – friendship, filial affection, military alliance, sex, duty to the sovereign, duty to the nation – are all made subservient to his own desire for power and wealth.

In the other story, Lear finds out that the two daughters he gave his lands to object to him staying at their houses with his retinue of a hundred men. They demand of him to reduce their number or, rather, give them up altogether. Enraged and maddened, Lear heads out into the night, the storm and the cold accompanied by his jester, the Fool. During this bitter, crazy, furious descent from king to destitute, we become involved in action and debate around the purpose of the bonds between parents and children, aristocrats and their followers and servants. Lear, supposedly in favour of the old order, has in fact broken with it by throwing out Cordelia and Kent – not that he realises this. As his knowing but cynical daughter Regan says of Lear early on in the play, 'he hath ever but slenderly known himself' – unlike the new order such as Regan herself, her sister and Edmund, who know precisely what their own motives are.

So in the middle of the storm, the once great all-powerful Lear says this:

'Poor naked wretches, whereso'er you are,
That bide the pelting of this pitiless storm,
How shall your houseless heads and unfed sides,
Your loop'd and window'd raggedness, defend you
From seasons such as these?'

Here is the arrogant ex-king, of all people, asking how the poor cope. That's the poor who are without houses,

unfed, their ragged clothes full of holes and openings
['loop'd and window'd'].

'O I have ta'en

Too little care of this. Take physic, Pomp;

Expose thyself to feel what wretches feel,

That thou may'st shake the superflux to them,

And show the Heavens more just.'

[Take physic, Pomp' = take medicine, royal authority, ie, cure yourself]

Lear is shouting at himself (as someone who was once Pomp personified), but as this is a play, Shakespeare, through Lear, is shouting these words to all pomp. And what is being said here is that monarchs should feel what the poor feel so that they will redistribute some of their surplus wealth to them *['shake the superflux'].*

Interestingly, almost as if Shakespeare was worried that we might have missed this, later in the play Gloucester, also at the end of his tether, humbled, destitute and mutilated, says something very similar. He, face to face with someone he thinks is a mad, poor beggar but is in fact his loyal son, says:

'Here, take this purse, thou whom the heav'ns' plagues

Have humbled to all strokes.'

(ie, you who the heavens' plagues have humbled into taking the worst strokes of fortune)

'…that I am wretched

Makes thee the happier: Heavens, deal so still!

Let the superfluous and lust-dieted man,

That slaves your ordinance, that will not see
Because he does not feel, feel your power quickly;
So distribution should undo excess,
And each man have enough.'

(ie, I am wretched so that makes you better off than I am. Let the heavens go on treating us that way. Let the rich man, who is well fed on his lusts and desires – he who enslaves heaven's commands, he who does not see because he has no human feeling – let him feel heaven's power. This way, sharing out wealth should get rid of excess and each man have enough.)

Back with Lear, in his destitute state, his mind hectically running over his life, his decisions, his failure as a ruler, he comes across someone he thinks is poor, naked and mad, but who is in fact the legitimate son, Edgar, in disguise and in flight, as Poor Tom. This tips him into a state of madness in which he sees the contrast between civilised man, dressed and sheltered, and naked Tom exposed to the elements:

'Is man no more than this? Consider him well. Thou
ow'st *[owe]* the worm no silk, the beast no hide, the
sheep no wool, the cat no perfume…thou art the thing
itself; unaccommodated man is no more but such a
poor, bare, forked animal as thou art.'

It's one of the great moments in world theatre: the great and powerful comes face to face with the real existence of humanity without the trappings of wealth. And it stuns the mighty into a kind of mad, beautiful, insightful poetry. As 21st century people, we might well come up with different solutions to the poverty that Lear finds, different from shaking a bit of royal superflux around while keeping the system intact. But that's beside the point. At one level, your heart and emotions may well be feeling wrung dry watching the human and personal dramas meeting their point of crisis here. At another level, what's so stunning, seeing and hearing these words and actions, is realising that you are watching the crisis of Tudor and Stuart monarchical government unfolding in front of you.

In another scene we are drawn into the depths of depravity the new order will go to to secure its position. Gloucester has his eyes taken out by Regan and her husband Cornwall. Again, sitting in the theatre we can feel blown away by the horror and injustice of this while at the same time feeling a sense that you are looking at late 16th century, early 17th century history being told to you by someone who lived then. The Tudor way of dealing with the old order, if it refused to accept the Tudor version of state religion, was to hunt down, torture, mutilate and execute. It's very hard to imagine that anyone watching the play would not have made some kind of analogy between the torturing and eventual death of Gloucester with the Tudors' persecution of the Roman Catholic aristocracy.

In a strange way, watching the play can seem like waves of horror and tragedy rolling over you. At various times you might easily think that you've reached some kind of conclusion, but as Goneril's husband Albany warns Goneril, us and the world:

'If that the heavens do not their visible spirits
Send quickly down to tame these vile offences
It will come,
Humanity must perforce prey on itself
Like monsters of the deep.'

Even though he's compromised by being part of the Goneril-Regan camp, he can see the forthcoming human disaster if the vile offences of the new order aren't tamed. The implication of Shakespeare's play is that the new order needed to be tamed with the values of the old. We might think differently today. Lear himself in his 'mad-sane' outbursts conjures up images of corruption, self-revelation and heartbreaking loss. In one extraordinary speech he froths furiously and sarcastically about sex and sin, saying, it seems, that the new, so-called rational crowd who are destroying the old values become slaves to uncontrolled animal desire: 'Down from the waist they are Centaurs *[ie animal]*, though women all above.' And yet in saying this, and cursing it, he sounds absorbed and corrupted by it.

'Beneath *[ie in the genitals]* is all the fiend's *[belonging to*

the devil]; there's hell, there's darkness,
There is the sulphurous pit – burning, scalding,
Stench, consumption; fie, fie, fie! Pah, pah!'

To see the play is to feel saddened, perhaps overwhelmed by the reunions, deaths and destruction in the closing moments, but one of the reasons why it can feel so unbearable is, I would argue, that Lear himself comes to such devastatingly punchy revelations about how society operates. In emotional and dramatic terms he cures himself of his arrogant, self-satisfied certainties. He's discovered or rediscovered the charitable, caring origins of the old order, so, we might feel, shouldn't he live? By casting the play as a tragedy with its inevitable deaths, it's hard to escape the conclusion that Shakespeare was ringing the death-knell on that class outlook, even as he appears to reaffirm its right to exist in its cleaned-up, reformed shape. Four hundred years after the following lines were written, it seems amazing that Shakespeare had the nerve to put words like these into the mouth of an old king of England:

'Look with thine ears,' he says to the blind Gloucester, 'see how yond justice rails upon *[shouts at]* yond simple thief. Hark, in thine ear; change places, and, handy-dandy *[hey presto]*, which is the justice, which is the thief? Thou hast seen a farmer's dog bark at a beggar?

Gloucester: Ay sir.

Lear: And the creature run from the cur? There thou might'st behold
The great image of Authority:
A dog obey'd in office.
Thou rascal beadle, hold thy bloody hand!
Why dost thou lash that whore? Strip thine own back. [You want to use the whore for the same thing that you're punishing her for]
Thou hotly lusts to use her in that kind
For which thou whipp'st her.
The usurer hangs the cozener. [The unscrupulous money-lender sentences the cheat to death]
Thorough tatter'd clothes small vices do appear;
Robes and furr'd gowns hide all. Plate sin with gold
And the strong lance of justice hurtless breaks;
Arm it in rags, a pigmy's straw does pierce it.' [thorough = through]
(Give sin an armour made of gold, and justice, as if it were a strong lance, merely breaks. Give sin the protection of nothing more than rags, and a tiny straw can pierce it – ie, one law for the rich, one law for the poor, or what Jeffrey Archer thought he was entitled to.)

I want now to look at three more plays. I'll do this more briefly as I want to give more of an idea of the kind of variety of issues and tones that Shakespeare develops across the plays. So I'll look at a comedy, *Twelfth Night*, a 'romance', *The Tempest*, and a historical play, *Coriolanus*. This doesn't give the full range of his plays by any means and is meant to encourage anyone reading this to find a way to seeing, performing or at least reading many more of the plays.

Shakespearean comedy doesn't always make the journey from Shakespeare's times to now very easily. There are good and bad reasons for this. Good reasons are that the verbal gags often turn on words, phrases and references that have lost their meaning, and the need for the jokes, in terms of targets worth having a go at, may have become less sharp. Bad reasons include a tendency by modern productions to insert all kinds of actors' 'business' as part of a nervousness about the obscurity of the wit.

Twelfth Night is a play that involves a series of disguises and deceptions, which in turn lead to people making errors over the matter of who any person thinks they are talking to. So, for example, the middle class (but not ennobled) twins Viola and Sebastian are shipwrecked in Illyria but each imagines that the other is dead. Viola dresses as a man (Cesario) so that she can gain access to the local aristocrat's mansion, but in the complicated misunderstandings later in the play people think that this Viola-Cesario person is Sebastian and Sebastian is Viola-Cesario. The play's humour relies on the speed with which all these and the other deceptions become intertwined and dangerous for the people concerned. As the clown, Feste, observes at one point, 'Nothing that is so, is so.'

This kind of farce (and possibly all farces) work as crazy extensions of real life. In real life we frequently make mistakes of identification, misjudgements of appearance, misnamings and the like. So, for example, parents are renowned for calling their offspring's new lover by the name of his or her ex. There is both humour and danger in these moments and, indeed, the ghastly story of gangland rivalries has sometimes involved killing 'the wrong guy'. So getting identities wrong is seen as an everyday mistake. In Elizabethan London there were plenty of reasons for it to be similarly a matter for laughter and/or danger.

Marriage among the aristocracy and the aspiring middle classes was still a matter of matching and arranging. A theme that runs right through writing from Elizabethan times onwards centres on the anxiety of the rich and the 'better off' that an impoverished imposter might con his or her way into marrying into their family. In Shakespeare's time the anxiety about such matters must have been reaching a level never before experienced. The new rich were desperately trying to become titled, while the impoverished gentry were trying to get hold of the wealth of the new rich, while not relinquishing their 'nobility'. For those outside of such ghastly manoeuvrings, whether it's the so rich they don't care, or the poor who feel entitled to enjoy gags at their masters' expense, it's a matter of comedy and spectacle.

A more serious side to the matter of identity in Shakespeare's England was the matter of spying. It was a matter of life and death if you were identified as someone not loyal to the throne or the Church of England, or if you were a thief, a deserter or a mutineer. In a society without identity papers, passports and the like, and with plenty of people with scores to settle from previous plots, mutinies, conspiracies and wars, there must have been hundreds if not thousands of cases of deliberately falsified identification leading to wrongful imprisonment, torture and execution.

Twelfth Night and plays like it offer audiences what can be called 'anxious laughter' – a laughter born out of a mix of gratitude that it hasn't happened to me, pleasure at other people's misfortunes, surprise at the unexpected, and delight in the success in showing that other people (apart from yourself) can be conned, thereby proving that you are at the very least no more foolish than the next person. The dangerous side of wrong identification is represented in the play *(1)* with the captain of the wrecked ship, who will, if found by the authorities, be imprisoned or executed and *(2)* when the knockabout duelling between the ninny knight Sir Andrew Aguecheek, the sozzled knight Sir Toby Belch and Viola-Cesario draws in the capable, potentially lethal swordsman Sebastian, her twin brother.

Another kind of anxious laughter is explored when the mourning, dutiful lady of the gentry, Olivia, finds that she has fallen hopelessly in love with Viola-Cesario.

Meanwhile the mournful, effete, aristocratic gent, Orsino, seems to half-fancy the same person. A glorious riff on hetero and same-sex love plays with our own sexual natures, whatever they might be. (As is often pointed out, in Shakespeare's time Viola and Olivia would have been played by boys, so there are times when the boy playing Olivia is speaking passionate words to the boy playing Cesario who is in reality a boy, disguised as a woman, disguised as a man. We have no way of knowing if this added to the laughter, but it seems as if there was a good chance of it.)

There was an enemy to this kind of sexual fun. It came in the form of the reformers within the Protestant tendency of Christianity. Every religion in the history of all religions has thrown up at times of crisis and change its reformers who want to 'get back' to something that they identify as its uncorrupted, pure essence. In 16th and 17th century Europe these reformers gave themselves or were given many names, including Anabaptist, Calvinist, Hussite, Puritan and Brownist (the last two being named in *Twelfth Night*). Today the inheritors of these traditions can be found in Christian sects such as the Free Presbyterians and the Plymouth Brethren, but also in restrictive, controlling and shaming attitudes to sex, drugs and rock'n'roll.

Shakespeare had good reason to hate the Puritans. They were powerful in London government and did all they could to close down theatres and any kind of seasonal fun and games or carnival. (Of course, if all that the Puritans were was dull killjoys we would never have heard of them. It is to Puritans and their ilk, and not the pleasure-seeking Catholics (English or Roman), that we owe what democracy we have in western and northern Europe – and thence to the US and Australia.)

In *Twelfth Night* the Puritan enemy is Malvolio, who is a 'steward', ie a site manager, housekeeper and bursar for the Countess Olivia's mansion. She we might assume is of a similar tendency, particularly as she is mourning her brother's death so dutifully. Malvolio is loathed by the sponging, decadent drunken uncle of Olivia (Sir Toby Belch) and Olivia's maidservant (Maria), and these two suck in the fool (Feste), a rich wastrel rural knight (Sir Andrew Aguecheek), and another house-servant (Fabian) into deceiving and baiting the Puritan Malvolio. When the deception is acted well, this can be devastatingly funny. Much of it turns on Malvolio's hypocrisy – the very person who despises drunken, licentious behaviour and the pleasures of the body is conned into muttering to himself obscene references to peeing and a woman's fanny as he tries to decipher a false letter. It's this letter that deceives him into thinking that the Countess Olivia loves him, he who is no more than her servant and steward. The depth of the conflict is represented by the drunken uncle, Sir Toby Belch, when he shouts at Malvolio, 'Dost thou think, because thou art virtuous, there shall be no more cakes and ale?'

This phrase means what it means, but it also had a massive resonance with its contemporary audience because 'cakes and ale' was the familiar name for the parties and wild goings-on in and around churchyards on festive occasions. The 'cakes and ale' in question were the presents that the old local nobility gave to the peasantry as part of its 'protection'. It was a custom of the old order and very much opposed by the Puritans because it led to drunkenness, sex and less efficient working practices (!). Puritan-inclined ministers banned 'cakes and ale' from their churches.

So though *Twelfth Night* is a play whose texture and plotting rely on the issues of deception over and over again, the motives for and the outcomes of the deceptions involve other considerations. My view of the play is that it shows us people at different levels in society doing whatever they can to satisfy their appetites. The opening line is spoken by a lovesick aristocrat (Duke Orsino) who, though he sees himself as an expert on love, and claims to be in love, does nothing about actually meeting and talking to the woman in question. The line is the famous 'If music be the food of love, play on.' His love is, then, a kind of narcissistic non-touchy-feely love, full of flowery phrases. It's a love that can't lead to reproduction because it's so cerebral. If the aristocracy are all like this they will die out. This is matched at the outset by the Countess Olivia, who can't love because her brother has died. For these two their route to real pleasure of the body, sex, pleasure, energy and reproduction is cut off. Another side of this layer of the middle class (who, when titled with a 'sir' or a 'countess', are usually described as 'the gentry') is seen with Sir Toby Belch and the un-sexual man he is sponging off, Sir Andrew Aguecheek. Belch is utterly intent on getting hold of money so that he can spend it on booze and he's quite happy to con his 'friend', Sir Andrew, into giving it to him. Though Belch fancies Maria the maid-servant as part of his general 'grab pleasure quick' attitude, his pleasure too is in a cul-de-sac of alcoholic self-destruction. Belch and gang get a good deal of pleasure in the baiting of the seemingly anti-pleasure person, Malvolio, but even this runs out of steam and turns sour. Aguecheek, we see over and over again, is unable to be sexual in any way at all. He misunderstands what it means to 'accost' a woman, and wistfully looks back to a time when he was 'adored once'. His supposed 'wooing' of Olivia is a mere shell, and is only continuing because Belch is deceiving him that Olivia is interested in him. Meanwhile the lower middle class Malvolio is repression personified, for both in secret and when unlocked it's clear that he fancies both Olivia and Maria, but himself most of all.

The exciting and, in the end, most fulfilling pursuits of

pleasure come from the two main women, Olivia (when her sexual energies are aroused by Viola-Cesario) and Viola (who fancies the pants off Duke Orsino). For most of the play the route to satisfying these pleasures is blocked off – Olivia is in love with someone who is in reality a woman, and Viola can't declare her love for Orsino because she's pretending to be his manservant. This gives Shakespeare a great opportunity to show us Viola nearly revealing her womanhood, either to stem the flow of Olivia's passion towards her or because she wants to say to Orsino that she's hot for him. For much of the play this pent-up sex desperately needs to be satisfied, but all is saved by Olivia's twin brother Sebastian, so enabling Olivia to grab him lustfully, and for Viola to whip off her disguise and have Orsino after all.

If such fun leads somewhere other than the sheer pleasure of the moment in watching it, it's surely in the direction of how Shakespeare possibly imagined that the old aristocracy and the gentry class just below it could keep or revive its energy. Not by behaving like Orsino (with effete non-reproductive sex), nor like Olivia at the outset (weighed down with dutiful celibacy), nor like Belch and Aguecheek getting pissed, getting a rise out of baiting the new Puritan lower middle class and sponging off each other. Reviving and sustaining their position might come about, the play suggests to me, by releasing the sexual energies of middle class women. It's not something we necessarily have to agree with in some ideological sense, but to watch the machinations and arguments reveals the moment of change in society. The status quo at the opening of the play would, if allowed to continue, lead to sterility and decay. The arrival of the untitled (ie middle class) Viola on the scene sets everything in motion, the very motion of the classes in Shakespeare's society. Her arrival in what used to be called 'society' (ie upper middle class life) is underlined by the fact that she arrives from a shipwreck with virtually nothing. I'm arguing here that this is, in a way, a symbol of the way the new 'middling sort' appeared as if they had arrived with next to nothing into London's 'society'. Viola 'marries up' to the level of a duke. Meanwhile the potency of these new people is represented by the fact that middle class Sebastian, Viola's brother, defeats the decaying gentry-man, Sir Toby Belch, in a swordfight before winning the gentry-woman Olivia from the layer in society above his.

The Tempest is a play that is grouped with those plays of Shakespeare's that are thought of as resembling fairy stories. The central, all-important character is Prospero. He is a deposed duke who escaped, thanks to his people, from his dukedom in a boat with his daughter Miranda. When the action of play begins he is the sole master of an island. As luck would have it, he's conjured up a storm with his magical arts so that his usurper brother, the king who gave the usurper his dukedom, the king's son and various crew members become shipwrecked on Prospero's island.

The play recounts the working through of Prospero's plans and schemes to create a better world for him and his daughter, and this involves him controlling and thwarting other people's actions and desires. At first glance the play can easily feel like a megalomaniac's dream, and indeed Prospero is not only a magician but also what these days we would call an enlightened despot. Or, put another way, if we thought enlightened despotism was the best way to run society we could easily feel affirmed by what we see in the play.

But, as always with Shakespeare, the route to get to these generalities is full of contradiction and, for the sake of the drama, and the dialectic of the drama, full of other voices, other views, other outlooks, other kinds of action. One area up for dispute and action is the issue of servitude and slavery. There are four kinds of serving person on the island: Ariel, who is Prospero's loyal slave; Caliban, who is the island's rebellious field-slave; Trinculo, who is a jester to the shipwrecked aristocrats; and Stephano, who is described as their butler. As part of the process of bringing about the ideal circumstances of a perfect, legitimated dukedom, Prospero has to use his powers over his slaves. This he does by promising the loyal Ariel that he will eventually have his freedom, by repressing the rebellious field-slave, and by stamping out the rebellion that unites Caliban with Trinculo and Stephano. He is also seen to control the love-matching of his daughter by marrying her up a notch to the king's son, and to disempower the usurper and his ally the king's brother.

Shakespeare puts into the mouth of Caliban some of the most powerful and beautiful words he ever conjured up. On the one hand it identifies Caliban with the 'natural' poetry of nature (if that doesn't sound odd), but on the other it gives voice to a legitimate sense of grievance. We hear from Caliban the voice of the dispossessed as powerfully as we ever hear it in literature until the dispossessed themselves come to be heard. Here he is being of 'nature':

'Be not afeard,' he says to Trinculo and Stephano, 'the isle is full of noises,
Sounds and sweet airs, that give delight and hurt not.
Sometimes a thousand twangling instruments
Will hum about mine ears; and sometimes voices
That, if I then had waked after long sleep,
Will make me sleep again; and then, in dreaming,
The clouds methought would open, and show riches
Ready to drop upon me, that when I waked
I cried to dream again.'

Sadly, Caliban is often played as some kind of ballscratching, leery idiot, the untamed savage, as Prospero thinks of him. This nearly always means that these lines sound as if they're being uttered in a drain by a Millwall football fan. The justification for this is that Caliban is 'of the earth'. When he curses his slave-master he does so with the curses of nature asking, for example, that:

'All the infections that the sun sucks up
From bogs, fens, flats, on Prosper fall, and make him
By inch-meal a disease!'

Ariel, on the other hand, because he is loyal, is sometimes played by a woman as an ethereal (ie aerial) delightful being. There is enough scope in the play, as we can see from this speech, to give Caliban as much humanity as Shakespeare and his best contemporaries might imagine that a native non-European people could possess.

In his first main speech, though, Shakespeare allows Caliban to articulate a sense of injustice:

'This island's mine, by Sycorax my mother,
Which thou tak'st from me. When thou cam'st first
Thou strok'st me, and made much of me, would'st give me
Water with berries in't, and teach me how
To name the bigger light, and how the less,
That burn by day and night. And then I loved thee,
And showed thee all the qualities of th'isle,
The fresh springs, brine-pits, barren places and fertile.
Cursed be that I did so! All the charms
Of Sycorax – toads, beetles, bats light on you!

For I am all the subjects that you have,
Which first was mine own king; and here you sty me
In this hard rock, whiles you do keep from me
The rest o'th'island.'

So Prospero, who the power of the drama seems to be asking us to admire and support, achieves his ends by stepping on the backs of the native people. Maybe not such an enlightened despot in our eyes today, as we thought! So even as Shakespeare shows us someone claiming what is legitimately his, ie Prospero's claim on his dukedom, beneath him is someone saying the same about his 'kingdom', the island.

Elsewhere in the play, as the shipwrecked courtiers wander around the desert island, one old councillor summons up another vision of society.

Here it is uninterrupted by the usurpers:
'Had I the plantation of this isle, my lord
And were the king on't, what would I do?

[traffic = trade]
I'th'commonwealth, I would by contraries
Execute all things. For no kind of traffic
Would I admit, no name of magistrate.

[service = servants]
Letters should not be known. Riches, poverty,

[bourn = boundary]
And use of service, none. Contract, succession,

[tilth = area under cultivation]
Bourn, bound of land, tilth, vineyard, none.
No use of metal, corn, or wine, or oil.
No occupation; all men idle, all.

And women innocent too, but innocent and pure
No sovereignty –
All things in common nature should produce
Without sweat or endeavour. Treason, felony,
Sword, pike, knife, gun, or need of any engine
Would I not have; but nature should bring forth
Of its own kind all foison, all abundance,   *[foison =*
To feed my innocent people.   *profusion]*
I would with such perfection govern, sir,
T'excel the Golden Age.'

This is a male, labourless utopia, in which nature offers up its surplus without needing any work. Gerrard Winstanley, the English Revolution's most articulate socialist, writing only 30 or so years after Shakespeare, envisioned a 'common treasury for all', but he was realistic enough to know that it would involve very hard work. Gonzalo can only see this commonwealth as ruled by him, rather as Prospero runs his despotic kingdom. Even so, Gonzalo offers us a kingdom without servants in contrast to Prospero's rule.

The matter of servitude reaches its head in a comic-tragic revolt by Caliban and the aristocrats' servants. It peters out in drunkenness with Caliban being the articulate one, demanding of his European allies to leave the booze alone – 'do the murder first'. Before that, he took these Europeans to be gods, something that he learns to regret in the petering out of the rebellion.

The Tempest is a play that has come in for the 'poetic' treatment in a big way. Because Shakespeare has filled the play with musical speech, cascades of imagery, it seems to have given licence for some commentators and directors to treat it as if it is some kind of symbolic symphony, a game with pretty pictures. Yet again, this drains Shakespeare of his efforts to engage with us on questions of how should we live, how should we govern ourselves, how should we be governed. It seems to me that the debate can only get off the ground if we give Caliban in particular a chance to be as human as Shakespeare allows, rather than only as human as Prospero allows.

The fact that Shakespeare was writing at the moment of colonial settlement of places like the Caribbean, when the fruits of slavery and material plunder were flooding into London, makes the dramatic encounter between the all-powerful, all-knowing tamer of the elements Prospero and the native people Ariel and Caliban all the more intense. Even though the rebellion is abortive, the mere fact that it involved an alliance between the natives and the European servants is something that we don't see in literature for many years.

Finally, let's look at one other rebellion.

In 1649, a group of middle class men, chosen by people of a similar background, tried and executed King Charles I. Some 40 or so years earlier Shakespeare wrote a play in which a group of middle class men, chosen by people of a similar background, assassinated the king, Julius Caesar. In Shakespeare's play, the immediate response is, 'Liberty! Freedom! Tyranny is dead! Run hence, proclaim, cry it about the streets.' I've often thought that for Shakespeare to have thought that this was worth putting on the stage in the early 1600s, he must have had a sense that this kind of talk was in the air. Sadly, much of what is written about Shakespeare's plays, even the most obviously political, drains them of their politics. It's easily done if you describe the conflicts in general terms (eg good versus evil), if you focus purely on the imagery of the plays, or if your political references are limited to small pieces of contemporary politicking around the monarch.

We have to bear in mind that within one lifetime of Shakespeare's writing there was a revolution in England that drew into its turmoil almost everyone. The causes of that revolution lay in the society Shakespeare lived in and wrote about. It was a time of high anxiety, focused in part on the figure of Elizabeth herself – who would succeed someone who had no children? But in a way that focusing was a metaphor for general anxiety about such things as: how should a country be governed; how might political power belong to those with wealth, instead of simply being something that is inherited; how can people's basic needs for food and shelter be met, when clearly poverty, disease and death are rife? One of the plays that raises these questions is *Coriolanus*.

This time, I shall avoid the path I've taken so far in writing about the plays, which was to try and get to some important meanings of the play as a whole. Instead, I'll keep the purpose of this book in mind by making this section more of a 'tease'. Opening scenes in Shakespeare are amazing demonstrations of dramatic skill, with their setting up of action, ideas, conflict and oppositional viewpoints. I'll look at what happens in the opening moments in *Coriolanus* with a view to whetting appetites for anyone reading this either to revisit the play, or to see it, read it, or perform it for the first time.

The scene opens with a group of workers and artisans appearing before us, armed with whatever weapons they can lay their hands on. It's clear they are angry and in revolt. One of them (only identified in the script as 'First Citizen'), speaks to them:

[famish = starve]

'You are all resolved rather to die than to famish?'

…you know Caius Martius is chief enemy to the people?

Let us kill him, and we'll have corn at our own price.'

This is the first time we hear of this 'Caius Martius'. The crowd support the First Citizen loudly and clearly. He goes on:

[patricians = wealthy men]

'We are accounted poor citizens, the patricians good.

What authority surfeits on would relieve us. If they would yield us but the superfluity *[surplus]* while it were wholesome, we might guess they relieved us humanely; but they think we are too dear: the leanness that afflicts us, the object of our misery, is an inventory to particularise their abundance; our sufferance is a gain to them. Let us revenge this with our pikes, ere we become rakes. For the gods know, I speak this in hunger for bread, not in thirst for revenge.'

[The surplus that the ruling class lives off would relieve our hunger and poverty]
[Our poverty is like a catalogue that itemises their wealth]
[before we become as thin as rakes]

This is clearly no silly caricature of a rebel leader. He is to the point, witty (with his gag about pikes and rakes) and, more importantly, he makes the economic analysis – they've got a surplus while we starve. They also have a plan of action – kill the person they think responsible, Caius Martius, an act which they think will cause the patricians to treat them more humanely.

The next moment in the scene is an open-ended discussion as to whether Caius Martius's actions on the battlefield on behalf of the nation should be praised. We see here immediately that these workers are by no means as resolute in their hatred of the man when asking themselves this kind of politico-*military* question rather than the politico-*economic* ones.

A moment later we hear that the workers in another part of the city have 'risen' too.

Then onto the stage comes someone called Menenius Agrippa, identified by one of the citizens as someone who has 'always loved the people', and we hear from his speech (both in style and content) that he is a patrician, or in Elizabethan terms, a middle class member of parliament.

This Menenius urges the men to stop or they'll 'undo' themselves.

[undone = ruined] 'We cannot, sir, we are undone already,' says the First Citizen.

Menenius says:

'I tell you, friends, most charitable care
Have the patricians of you.'

(You can imagine in a production the citizens jeering at this!)

'For your wants,
Your suffering in this dearth *[time of poverty]*, you may as well
Strike at the heaven with your staves, as lift them
Against the Roman state, whose course will on
The way it takes…
For the dearth
The gods, not the patricians, make it…'

(Last time I heard someone make that point it was Margaret Thatcher's chancellor of the exchequer, Nigel Lawson!)

He goes on:

'…you slander
The helms o'th'state, who care for you like fathers,
When you curse them as enemies.'

So by now, only a few minutes into the play, we're seeing some political faultlines: there are the hardliners who see things in class terms, who blame the poverty on Caius Martius and want to rise up and kill him; there are the wobblers who think that may be a good plan, but Caius Martius is a great general and served the nation well, so perhaps they might be prepared to sacrifice their class interests for the national interest; and there's the patrician who claims that poverty is god-made and that the ruling class are like fathers to the people.

The First Citizen is scathing in his reply:

'Care for us? True indeed! They ne'er [*never*] cared for us yet. Suffer us to famish, and their store-houses crammed with grain; make edicts for usury, to support usurers; repeal daily any wholesome act established against the rich, and provide more piercing statutes daily, to chain up and restrain the poor. If the wars eat us not up, they will; and there's all the love they bear us.'

It's an amazing speech. Grain-hoarding became a crime in Elizabethan England, as it was understood that it pushed up the price of bread. Familiar too was the idea that people in parliament, supposedly there to defend people against 'usury' (ie high interest rates on loans) passed laws [*'edicts'*] that made it easy for banks to be set up (which of course charged interest). Similarly, while acts were being passed to make money-making easier, tough laws against 'vagabondage' and 'beggary' were passed too. Then, as for wars, the Elizabethan period was one of virtually non-stop war, decimating the poor. If anyone were to write a Marxist history of the period, the First Citizen's speech would be as good a place to start as any!

If you don't know the play, then perhaps you might have a guess at some of the issues and actions that might arise from all this. I'll say no more here other than to say that there is a scene in the middle of the play in which Caius Martius – later to be called Coriolanus – confronts the representatives of the people. For anyone who has read (or heard on radio) the Putney Debates, the arguments between the propertied anti-democrats and the unpropertied democrats within Cromwell's army, then Shakespeare offers us a staggeringly similar debate, laced with all the drama and danger of revolt, class war, foreign war and counter-revolution.

FOUR: *Shakespeare today*

SHAKESPEARE'S PLAYS DON'T COME TO us from 400 years ago through some kind of hermetically sealed tunnel. We always receive them, watch them and read them in a context – or, to be more accurate, various contexts – the society we live in, the institutions through which we find Shakespeare like school, the entertainment industry, and so on. Each and every one of these contexts has its own traditions and history. So if we do the most obvious thing, which is go to a theatre to see one of the plays, what we're doing is taking part in an institution, the theatre, that has a particular kind of status in society, a particular kind of hierarchy, a particular kind of flavour. Similarly, if we ask ourselves why we went to that theatre to watch Shakespeare then there'll be reasons to be found, in the status that Shakespeare has in our lives, whether that's a result of schooling, home background, or meetings with significant people and groups of people in our lives. All this is by way of saying that when we meet Shakespeare, we do so carrying our own baggage, only to find that Shakespeare himself is carrying even more.

In an ideal world this would be no more than a passing comment. Sadly, we live in a society where much of Shakespeare's baggage smells and our own baggage can weigh so heavy we never feel like bothering to meet him anyway. I'll give some examples. In school there is a contradiction between the way Shakespeare is put on a plinth as the world's greatest writer doing his bit to put the Great back into Britain, and the grinding curriculum constraints that are put on teachers who have to teach him. The result of this is that for many of us going through school Shakespeare can come to be some kind of elaborate crossword puzzle. We might sit in our places in class, struggling to understand each word, each line, each speech, so that at the end of that year we can get a good grade. The key to understanding, it might seem, lies with the teacher who knows more about Shakespeare than we do, so it's a good idea to shuttup and listen.

The tragedy here is that what Shakespeare wrote were scripts. The irony of that tragedy is that the scripts we have today are the way they are precisely because they were often written down by actors, 'pirates' who tried to remember what they saw and the men who prompted the actors when they forgot their lines. If Shakespeare is compulsory in schools, then we can say how strange that it's not compulsory to perform him! That tells you how deeply ingrained in us is the idea that Shakespeare belongs to the highly literate academic sitting in a study. Every Shakespeare play offers a multitude of possibilities for people to explore the ideas and meaning through performance. The scene in *Romeo and Juliet* where Capulet tries to bully Juliet into marrying Paris only comes to life when we have a sense that she is fresh from her love-making with Romeo and we have a sense of how the Nurse and Juliet's mother react to what's going on. The end of *King Lear* makes only one kind of sense on the page. For the ideas to matter, we have to experience either as performers or watchers the physical and visual transformation of Lear from 'great' king to destitute madman.

Again, it is criminal that Shakespeare is used by this society as a means by which we gain access (or not) to more education. He is recruited to stand as one of the gatekeepers segregating us into different kinds of jobs. Small wonder that people who feel that they have 'failed' their Shakespeare exam should be put off going to see the plays for the rest of their lives. It shouldn't be possible to fail Shakespeare – there should only be different ways to enjoy the plays. The good news is that there is a growing number of teachers who know this and appreciate this, and who organise to fight against the stultifying weight of tests, exams and the prescribed curriculum. They are a crucial part of what is our struggle to put Shakespeare into the hands of all the people who were put off or 'failed' Shakespeare.

Also involved here is saving Shakespeare from the flag. Shakespeare's life followed a progression from low status, lowlife activity into a high status, royally approved institution. The theatres that he started out working in were among modern Europe's first purpose-built arenas, but they were no more than wooden towers built among the whorehouses and rickety tenements outside the city walls – that is, beyond the jurisdiction of London's radical Protestant council that opposed theatre on the grounds that it encouraged sex, riot and plague. By the time he was in his forties, Shakespeare was a shareholder in the Globe; his company of actors and performers were the 'King's Men'; plays like *Macbeth* were being premiered in front of the monarch, James I; and Shakespeare himself was a big landowner, property owner and local tax collector. Following his death in 1616, the plays themselves fell into disuse and misuse until the late 19th century. For all these years they were read and much appreciated by no more than a tiny minority of writers and critics – people like Samuel Johnson, the person who put together the first good English dictionary, or John Keats the London poet. And it wasn't really until the film industry got hold of Shakespeare, with, say, Laurence Olivier in the 1940s and 50s or the so-called Marlon Brando version of *Julius Caesar* that the plays were seen by millions. Before that, though, something happened in British culture that has helped shape the way Shakespeare comes to us – the invention of 'English Literature' as a subject to study at school and university.

Terry Eagleton and others have shown how carving certain privileged books written in the British Isles off from European and world literature and turning them into material worthy of study was part of a national, quasi-religious struggle on the part of one section of the English literary elite. This carve-up not only denied the internationalism of all literature, as, like Shakespeare himself, it borrows and plagiarises and feeds into the pool of other literatures from all over the world. It also required *(1)* a suppressing of some writers, notably women and writers from working class popular traditions and *(2)* a filleting of the writers chosen for this nationalist project. Shakespeare had the sexy bits censored in school editions. A play like *Coriolanus* that gives voice to a rebellious working class never made it as a core text, and the courses of study drowned the politics, social texture and dynamism of the plays under hours of analysis of 'character', 'language', 'imagery' and so-called 'universal' themes.

Meanwhile, Shakespeare became 'royal' and 'national'. He is forever being co-opted by politicians, monarchs and their supporters as a representative of a united Britain. Just as it's claimed that the monarchy 'isn't political' (even as

people praise it for 'uniting the nation' and 'offering political stability'!), so Shakespeare is hauled into the same
arena. The consequence is that Shakespeare is seen as
'belonging' to such institutions as the two big showpiece
theatres, the Royal Shakespeare Theatre and the National
Theatre, the monarchy, the government's education and
exam boards, a certain kind of English accent, and that
part of the educated elite that supports the national and
royal implications of all this. While the big showpiece theatres receive massive state grants (and for that reason we
should avail ourselves of every opportunity to see the
shows they put on), the small local and touring companies
who want to take Shakespeare and Shakespeare work-
shops into schools, youth clubs, old people's homes, clubs
and the like face a nightmare of juggling sponsorship,
funding and work. Again, part of fighting to get hold of
Shakespeare and letting it speak to us is a struggle to get
the plays put on everywhere.

Of course, the irony in turning Shakespeare into a safe
national icon is that much of what he wrote, as we've seen,
is extremely *un*safe. Again and again, we see characters'
greed for power and money, we see hypocrisy and manipulation, we see the instability of institutions, we observe
fierce debates about how personal, sexual, social and political life should be run. That said, some radical critics have
noted that when you put the conclusions of Shakespeare's
plays together, as some kind of ideological picture, you

have a general sense of a caring conservatism – a sense that the old order has made mistakes and the new order is vicious, so let's have faith in love, duty, obedience, loyalty. It should be said here that it's pointless trying to figure out if this is what Shakespeare actually believed, or even that he pretended he believed so as to keep his royal patrons sweet. If all we have are the tiny fragments of contextual evidence that survive, we are either left with clever guess-work or analysis of what it feels like to act, see, hear and read the plays.

Plays are always much more than their endings, and in conventional theatre even more so. That's to say Shakespeare, along with most writers up until the 20th century, wrote within traditions that prescribed how, say, a 'comedy' should end – ie in marriage and unity; a 'tragedy' in death and a sliver of hope for the future, and so on. For all that, Shakespeare as much as anyone subverted and broke with the prescriptions, creating historical plays that weren't just 'chronicles' but were murderous debates, plays like *Measure for Measure* that were and are impossible to categorise according to the old labels. What's more, and this is even more important, Shakespeare's method is more important than his conclusions. His method is dialectic – what we see is a clash of outlooks and viewpoints in action. Famously, when he wanted to show the clash between the usurious Jew and the modern merchant, he had to humanise the socially hated figure of the Jew and put into his mouth what is one of the first humanistic attacks on anti-Semitism and racism ever heard. What's more, he shows us anti-Semitism and racism in action against the Jew, yes, victorious, but dubiously so. This means that part of the way we make Shakespeare ours is to engage in conversation, debate and argument about such things. We contest the certainties laid down by authority and let the plays work as inspirations for debate.

Another radical argument looks at Shakespeare's representation of the working class in the plays and finds him guilty of precisely the kind of stereotypes that make us yawn and despair at contemporary films and TV. In *Julius Caesar*, this argument says, workers are reduced to a fickle, dangerous mob, ripe for recruitment by demagogues and upper class republicans. In *A Midsummer Night's Dream* they are shown to be illiterate bumpkins, fawning at the feet of royalty. In the Henry IV plays they are not much more than drunken, whoring cannon-fodder. At best in the plays, the argument goes, they are not much more than wise-cracking servants with moments of social comment and what the Russian Marxist Bakhtin called 'subversive laughter', as you get with the grave-diggers in *Hamlet*, the nightwatchman figure in *Macbeth*, Pompey in *Measure for Measure* and, arguably, the jesters and fools such as Lear's fool and Feste in *Twelfth Night*.

In many ways, this is an unanswerable criticism. It's only

really in *Coriolanus*, the confused rebellion in *The Tempest* and in certain moments with Jack Cade the peasant rebel in the Henry VI plays that working class characters are given an independent voice, with space to voice their concerns. You can sit in a posh theatre and wonder exactly what you or the people around you are laughing at when the tinker, the bellows-mender, the joiner, the weaver and the rest chew to bits the Romeo and Juliet type story that they put on as a spectacle for the royals. There's a fine line in this kind of humour between what is at one level a mockery of romantic love, and what is a mockery of semi-literate workers. On the matter of this particular play (*A Midsummer Night's Dream*) Shakespeare offers us the possibility of dealing with the snobbery. The aristos who watch the workers' show make jokey comments on what they're watching. One way to play this is to support these comments as jolly witticisms. Another way (and Shakespeare's script has scope for it) is to play their comments as effete sneering, putting our own laughter into question.

I make this point in some detail because it is precisely the kind of dilemma that turning Shakespeare into living theatre poses. You have to deal with real people (actors, producers, stage crews) and audiences. Because, as I've said, the plays are dialectical, there is massive scope for interpretation, rereading, re-presenting the scripts we have. As theatre in action, whether it's in a classroom, church hall, community centre or posh theatre, this is where the plays really happen. However, there is an industry of scholarship that sits and debates the exact textual meaning of this or that phrase, or tries to find poetic, paradoxical and metaphorical links and themes through the plays. There are others who use the new tools of 'theory' to put the plays into specific theoretical, material, ideological and psychoanalytic contexts. I confess that all my life I've found much of this fascinating and sometimes insightful. Sometimes I've found it incomprehensible, intimidating and part of some closed game by which a specific cultural group finds ways of only talking within its own walls.

So, in spite of my concerns here, I'm not calling for an end to Shakespeare criticism – how could I, or should I? This book is part of it! This book, though, is offered as part of a tradition that tries to find Shakespeare in context and the context in Shakespeare, and in support of anyone wanting to do that by watching or playing Shakespeare live.

This takes us to now. No matter what leaps and bounds we might make in trying to feel the personal, social and political reality of Shakespeare's works, we can only ever do it with who we are now and where we are now. I don't take this argument so far as to say that there is no Shakespeare and that there is only your or my reading of Shakespeare. There is, in my view, some kind of 'transaction' that goes on between the reader/spectator and the performance/text/show. Though it is the 'I' that makes the meanings, these meanings are not totally down to the 'I's psyche, or even to his or her social formation. The text (here, the play) exists within certain boundaries of shared knowledge. It is not limitlessly reinterpretable (unless there are clear decisions to rewrite, cut and change – no bad thing in itself). What I'm saying here is that we come to accept certain basic structures of the texts like, say, that Hamlet's father has been killed by this dead man's brother. However, the 'I' that reads, spectates and makes meanings exists as part of social existence. The 'I' is, in effect, inseparable from a 'we', or many different kinds of 'we'.

What follows from this is that for anyone who cares about the idea of art being something that enables us to see the possibilities for all human beings to live in a better way than we do now, then seeing, performing, reading and talking about Shakespeare's plays is one of the ways that we can do this. This is the case not because Shakespeare lays down great ideas for creating a better society. It is because he shows us human beings acting from within their social circumstances, striving to change those circumstances. Though the conflicts that result from these strivings are embedded in Shakespeare's era, our own societies, all round the world, throw up similar and analogous situations and moments. Part of the way we enjoy books from the past inevitably involves us in making these comparisons. To see the savagery of a modern military politician in the ruthlessness and guilt of Macbeth is part of the fun. Likewise, to see the courage and desire of a young woman opposing her middle class parents in Juliet can give us hope. To watch the creepy hypocrisy of a repressed, authoritarian ruler trying to blackmail women into bed in *Measure for Measure* is to get insight into what goes on behind the scenes in the White House or in the minds of the Tory party's most famous jailbird. To do all this is to contest the rigid laying down of meanings that the education courses and textbooks often require us to do. We can and should work for these acts of recognition and comparison so that the plays can live for us now in our imperfect world, and help us oppose our lying, greedy, warmongering, power-crazed rulers and the repressive laws, rules and conventions with which they try to govern our lives.

A note on books

If you're interested in reading the plays then the Arden editions of the plays have the advantage of giving you at the bottom of every page very thorough explanations and translations of difficult passages. There is also an introduction to each play telling you about where Shakespeare got the storylines from, when and where the play was first put on, the problems of deciding which particular version of the play to publish, the particular historical events that were going on at the time the play was put on. There is also a kind of critical outline of the play where a critic says what he or she thinks the play is really about.

If you're thinking of putting on the plays you'll need one of the cheap and cheerful editions that aren't loaded down with all this, so that the actors can use the book as if it's a script. Then you can use the Arden edition for explanations.

If you're thinking of reading more widely, then there are quite literally thousands and thousands of books to choose from. My approach here is to use the internet search engine Google. The trick here, if you don't already know it, is to type in the word 'Shakespeare' and/or the name of a play and then type in a word on whatever aspect or critic or book interests you. So let's say you're interested in Hamlet and existentialism: type in 'Shakespeare Hamlet existentialism'. For a variation type in 'existentialist' or (in double quotes) "existentialist approach". You will get hundreds of sites, some of which will be notes for American college students – which are often very good and accessible – lecture notes from university lecturers with recommendations of books and so on. Typing in 'Shakespeare' (or the name of a play or eg 'tragedy' or 'comedy') and then, 'Marx' or 'Marxism' or 'Marxist' or "Marxist approach" brings up a huge and interesting set of readings. I find it useful to click on the word 'cached' that comes up along the bottom line of each site that comes up on the Google lists. A few minutes playing around in this way will find you almost anything you might want in connection with Shakespeare.

That said, there are two books I would recommend above all others for anyone interested in getting a handle on what were the changing historical conditions under which Shakespeare wrote. You can find both of them on www.amazon.co.uk and/or www.abebooks.com quite cheaply. Alternatively your local library can put out a special search for them.

Curtis C Breight, *Surveillance, Militarism and Drama in the Elizabethan Era* (Palgrave Macmillan, 1996)

This is a stunning account of the mix of despotism and infant imperialism running through Tudor times. Hamlet, the History and the Roman plays will never seem the same again!)

Lawrence Stone, *The Causes of the English Revolution 1529-1642* (Routledge, Kegan and Paul, 1972)
Pages 58 to 117 are the best summary of the Tudor regime that I know of and I would recommend it to anyone interested in grasping the politics of the debate at the heart of most of the plays. I found that, having read this, scene after scene in the plays started to come alive as fierce political and social debates rather than, as I had been told, the working through of 'character'.

You can buy both these books on the web secondhand from a search engine like www.bookfinder.com or through Amazon's used books section.

Also in the revolutionary portraits series from Redwords

John Coltrane

Jazz, racism and resistance

Martin Smith

I was an active participant in many of the events Martin writes about; this excellent book makes me think about many of them in a different way! I'm not sure I agree with everything Martin says – but that is the point of this book, it is meant to challenge our perceptions of music and the civil cights movement. I believe the same spirit can be found in the music of John Coltrane.

I recommend this book to both radicals and music fans alike.

McCoy Tyner

ISBN: 1 872208 22 3

£5.99

online at: www.bookmarks.uk.com

REDWORDS

www.redwords.org.uk